331.7   Abrams, Kathleen S.
ABR
         Guide to careers
         without college

$11.90

DATE			

D1126840

GUIDE TO
CAREERS WITHOUT COLLEGE

GUIDE TO CAREERS WITHOUT COLLEGE

KATHLEEN S. ABRAMS

ALTERNATIVES TO COLLEGE
FRANKLIN WATTS ■ 1988
NEW YORK ■ LONDON ■ TORONTO ■ SYDNEY

The author wishes to acknowledge the
usefulness of the *Occupational Outlook
Handbook* in the preparation of this book.

All photographs courtesy of Lawrence F.
Abrams, except for the following:
Sygma: p. 13 (Y. Manciet); Monkmeyer: pp. 14
(Hugh Rogers), pp. 23, 68 (Mimi Forsyth), 81
(Hugh Rogers); Taurus Photos: pp. 34 (Spencer
Grant), 48 (Eric Kroll), 93 (Shirley Zeiberg), 99
(Laimute E. Druskis); Bellevue Hospital:
p. 41; Control Data Corporation: p. 52.

Library of Congress Cataloging-in-Publication Data

Abrams, Kathleen S.
Guide to careers without college.

(Alternatives to college)
Bibliography: p.
Includes index.
Summary: Discusses rewarding careers which do not
require a college degree, in such fields as health care,
sales and marketing, and the building trades.
1. Vocational guidance—Juvenile literature.
[1. Occupations. 2. Vocational guidance] I. Title.
II. Series.
HF5381.2.A27   1988   331.7'02   88-5723
ISBN 0-531-10585-7

CONTENTS

GUIDE TO
CAREERS WITHOUT COLLEGE

1

ALTERNATIVE CAREERS—A GOOD WAY TO EARN A LIVING

Carrie would like to get a job when she graduates from high school. "I need a break from school," she tells her friend Dan. "I want to earn some money and be on my own."

But Dan wonders about this. "I'd like to go on to college," he says, "but I just can't afford four years of college. I hope I can get a good job without a college degree."

Are you undecided about what you should do when you graduate from high school? Are you, like Carrie, ready to go to work? But do you worry, like Dan, that you will not make a good living or find a challenging job without a college education?

People often think of a college education as the only path to career success. But the job market is changing so fast that many good jobs available today do not require a college degree. In fact, only two of the twenty fastest growing occupations compiled by the Bureau of Labor Statistics require four years of college. You can get a job as a computer service technician or a legal assistant without a college degree. The demand for different types of technicians is growing so fast that people cannot be trained quickly enough for these jobs.

Even though four years of college are not needed for many good jobs, most of the best jobs still require you to have some sort of specialized training or education. You may, for example, need a two-year associate degree from a junior college or technical institute. Any training you can get will help you obtain a job as a perfusionist, orthotist, or aquaculturist. Other careers with strange sounding names are also springing up.

In this book we look at some of the jobs that will be in great demand in the future. All of the jobs described have good points to recommend them. They may draw good salaries, provide excellent opportunities for advancement, be especially stable, or offer a great deal of variety during the workday. After reading this book you will have an idea of the types of jobs you can get without a college degree and know more about how to go about getting these jobs.

One book, however, cannot tell you about all the jobs available, nor can you predict from reading it what job will be the best for you. When you have some idea of what you want to do, make an appointment with your high school counselor or with a career counselor at your local vocational school or community college. This counselor can give you tests that indicate what jobs fit your personality best and point out careers in which you will be most successful.

You will spend a good deal of your life on the job. Choose your occupation wisely, and be willing to look beyond the traditional jobs to alternative careers in this exciting time of rapid job change.

2

TRAINING
FOR ALTERNATIVE
CAREERS

Ways of training for jobs in the next decade are as varied as the jobs themselves. Some of the most popular ways of getting job training are discussed in this chapter.

On-the-Job Training

One way to train for a job is through an on-the-job training program. Many businesses or companies will let you learn as you work, whereas others have special training programs. You may learn the "ropes" from an experienced employee or go through several months of formal training. Some people "jump right in," learning the job as they do it. Other people are hired, trained for a specific job, and then go to work. According to a survey taken by the Bureau of Labor Statistics, half of all those surveyed said that they had received some on-the-job training. For example, computer operators get training on the specific computer system used in their workplace. Salesclerks may also go through a brief training program to become familiar with the merchandise they are selling.

Apprenticeships

An apprenticeship program usually includes both on-the-job training and classwork, in a trade such as plumbing or carpentry. Sometimes you can complete your course work at home through correspondence courses, but often the classes are offered at a technical institute.

If you choose an apprenticeship, you will usually have to sign a contract with an employer. In the contract, the employer typically agrees to provide you with instruction and to pay you a salary that is usually one-half of a fully qualified worker's pay. In return, you agree to learn the trade and apply your skills to the employer's business. You will need about four years to complete an apprenticeship program.

For more information on apprenticeships, contact the Bureau of Apprenticeship and Training in your area. You can get the address from your local public library or from the state employment agency.

Military Service

Joining the military is another way for you to get training for an alternative career. To do this you should have a high school diploma, although exceptions are sometimes made. You also must pass a physical examination and take an Armed Forces Vocational Battery to help determine what kind of training best fits your abilities. Many people find the military an excellent source of training. Because the military needs workers in many of the same occupations as does the civilian work world, skills you learn

Skills learned in the military can help you qualify for civilian jobs.

in the military can often be transferred to civilian work life if you decide to leave the military. For example, you may train as a nurse, cook, or welder in the military and find a civilian job in your field when you leave the service.

The armed forces place a high priority on training and offer a variety of educational opportunities. Participants in the Tuition Assistance Program, for example, can study at accredited civilian schools while they are on active duty. The military pays up to 90 percent of the tuition for any of the courses you take when you are not on duty. The new GI bill also helps to fund your college education.

For more information about military training programs, contact your local recruiter, who is listed in the Yellow Pages of your telephone directory.

13

Marketable skills can also be learned at vocational schools and junior colleges.

One- and Two-Year Schools

One of the more usual ways of preparing for an alternative career is to attend a vocational school or community college. Also called technical institutes or junior colleges, these schools offer one- or two-year training programs. You can earn an associate degree by completing a two-year program and a diploma by completing a one-year program. Most technician jobs require a two-year associate degree. You can find a job as a skilled laborer with a one-year diploma from a vocational school.

Most vocational and technical programs prefer high school graduates, but a high school equivalency diploma usually serves the same purpose. Some training programs also have specific requirements, such as four years of high school math or courses in biology or chemistry. While you are still in high school, find out from your high school counselor what requirements are necessary to enter the training program of your choice.

FOR FURTHER READING

"Apprenticeship." *Occupational Outlook Quarterly,* Winter 1983, pp. 18–30.

Baxter, Neale. "Job Training for Enlisted Personnel in the Military." *Occupational Outlook Quarterly,* Fall 1983.

Cetron, Marvin, and Appel, Marcia. *Jobs of the Future: The 500 Best Jobs—Where They'll Be and How to Get Them.* New York: McGraw-Hill, 1985.

Chronicle Occupational Briefs. Moravia, N.Y.: Chronicle Guidance, 1987.

Feingold, Norman S. "Emerging Occupational Careers for Post-Industrial Society." *The Futurist,* February 1984, pp. 9–16.

Hopke, William E., ed. *The Encyclopedia of Careers and Vocational Guidance, VIII.* Chicago: Ferguson, 1984.

"Jobs of the Future." *U.S. News & World Report,* December 23, 1985, pp. 40–45.

U.S. Department of Labor, Bureau of Labor Statistics. *Occupational Outlook Handbook,* April 1984.

Weinstein, Bob. *140 High-Tech Careers.* New York: Macmillan, 1985.

Wolkomir, Richard. "Careers of the Future." *OMNI,* September 1985, pp. 74–80.

3

SALES AND MARKETING

"Get involved in extracurricular activities in high school. This involvement shows employers that you are motivated," Jeanette says. She was the advertising editor of her school newspaper. Her success in selling ads for the newspaper impressed the employer when she was interviewed for her first sales job.

Now Jeanette is a salesclerk in the fashion department of a large department store. She helps customers, rings up sales, and keeps her department neat and well stocked with merchandise. She enjoys keeping up with the latest fashions and helping people select clothes.

Jeanette has an associate degree in marketing from a technical institute, and she participated in an on-the-job training program to prepare for this job. Before going to work on the floor, Jeanette spent three evenings attending classes. There she learned how to work the cash register and make out credit slips for returned items. She also watched training tapes on how to help a customer and what to do if she finds someone shoplifting.

Jeanette, a sales clerk, enjoys
keeping up with fashions and
helping people select clothes.

While she is learning about the job Jeanette works part time, but eventually she will take over a full-time job. Jeannette knows she will have to keep learning if she wants to move up in her job. She is taking a class in sales persuasion offered by her company, and eventually Jeanette hopes to move into a job as a buyer or department supervisor. To reach this career goal Jeanette would go from her job as a salesclerk on straight salary to a job selling more expensive items such as carpeting or appliances on commission. From there she could be promoted to assistant manager and eventually to sales manager. It could take Jeanette about four years to reach her goal.

In the next 10 years, 4.8 million new jobs will open up in the retail trades. Workers in this field sell goods such as clothing and appliances to customers. They work in businesses ranging from sporting goods shops to drugstores. They may pump gas, stock grocery shelves, or wait on tables. Jobs in retail trade also include wholesale sellers who sell to retail stores. These sales reps sell goods such as food or clothing to buyers from retail stores, who in turn sell the product to their customers.

If you are looking for a field with guaranteed openings, consider the retail field. You will probably need no special training or skills to be considered for entry-level employment. Jeannette found her education in marketing helpful, but it was not a requirement for her job. Many high school students find part-time work in department stores or grocery stores. From these beginnings, they can work themselves into jobs with greater responsibility and better pay.

Although most retail jobs pay about minimum wage, you can work your way into better-paying positions. Retail buyers, for example, earn as much as $40,000 a year. Car dealers and furniture salespeople also earn good salaries.

One way to get more money in a retail job is to get additional training, as Jeanette is doing. Technical schools and junior colleges offer courses in marketing, and the larger department stores and chains have their own trainee programs.

The following sections describe a few jobs that are available in sales.

SALESCLERK

Salesclerks sell products, stock shelves, and take inventory. As a salesclerk your first goal is to sell the store's products. Patience and a friendly manner are appreciated in a salesclerk. Also, the more familiar you are with the products you sell, the better your chances are for success.

As a general rule, try to find a job in a store that sells things you would like to own yourself. Most salesclerks start out in stores selling inexpensive items such as shoes and costume jewelry.

Although "making those sales" can be rewarding, the job of salesclerk can also be tiring. You will be on your feet for hours at a time. When business is slow, the job may become tedious. You should also be prepared to work weekends, evenings, and holidays, since most stores stay open at these times to serve the increasing number of customers who can't shop during the regular working day. Some employees work a split shift—four hours in the morning and four in the evening.

Education and Training

You will need very little training to work as a salesclerk. When you are hired, the store manager will show you the store's routine and tell you how to ring up sales and deal with returns. The manager should also tell you about the merchandise that the store stocks.

Some salesclerks obtain a one-year diploma from a vocational school. They may also earn an associate degree in marketing. A clerk with a diploma in retail sales or an associate degree in marketing has a better chance for advancement.

Career Opportunities and Salary

Salesclerks in entry-level jobs usually earn minimum wage and work part time. As you gain experience, or if you go back to school for additional training, you may move into better sales jobs. People who sell expensive items such as boats, furniture, and computers usually work full time and earn a good hourly wage. They also earn commissions on the items that they sell. These commissions are a percentage of their total sales and can add greatly to their earnings. Salesclerks usually also receive discounts on merchandise that are sold in the stores in which they work.

RETAIL BUYER

Can you take risks? Are you good at figuring out what people want? Do you enjoy shopping? If so, you may enjoy a job as a retail buyer.

Buyers purchase merchandise for resale. They study shopping trends and buy products they think they can sell to their customers. Buyers attend "shows" where a group of wholesalers display their products. At these shows buyers purchase products for the best prices they can get.

They must be able to make decisions quickly and be comfortable with some risk because they can never be absolutely sure their store's customers will like the merchandise they select.

Retail buyers work in department stores and grocery stores; they also find jobs in drugstores, jewelry stores, and other smaller retail stores.

This fast-paced field usually involves a lot of traveling. People who seek jobs as buyers usually thrive on the activity; therefore, competition for these jobs can often be stiff.

Education and Training

You will need training or experience to be a buyer. Ideally, you should earn an associate degree in marketing or merchandising from a technical institute or junior college. This degree will give you the basics in buying, selling, and store management. It will also qualify you to enter a buyer trainee program offered at the store in which you work. Some salesclerks also work their way into buyer trainee programs. Each store trains its buyers to understand its particular needs. Saks Fifth Avenue, the May Company, Sears, and J. C. Penney are all department stores, but each carries its own selection of merchandise and caters to a particular kind of customer.

Career Opportunities and Salary

As a buyer you will have a good chance to move into jobs with better pay and more responsibility. For example, you could become a manager for a department store or chain store.

WHOLESALE-TRADE
SALES REPRESENTATIVE

Wholesale-trade sales representatives—called sales reps—sell manufacturers' products to retailers. They usually specialize in one type of product, such as clothing, food, or paper products, but they often sell many brands of that product.

Many sales reps work from offices in their homes. They call on customers and show them samples and catalogs. They take orders and refer those orders to distribution centers. Producers rely on reps to get their goods into the stores.

Wholesale-trade sales reps present new merchandise to buyers.

Wholesale sales has a lot of chance for growth, but it is also demanding. Sales reps put in long hours. They may cover one neighborhood of a large city or an entire state. They are often away from home for several days at a time. They usually "work out of their car" and often must load and unload heavy samples.

On the plus side, in wholesale sales you will usually see direct results from your hard work. The more sales calls you make and the better you present your product, the more sales you will generate. You can build a good career from a start in wholesale sales.

Education and Training

Most reps start in entry-level jobs in a company and work their way up. For example, you might start in the stockroom or shipping department, learn about the company, and then move into a selling job.

Often you can start in wholesale sales as soon as you graduate from high school. But some jobs require specialized training. For example, if you want to sell computers, you may find it helpful to have completed a data processing or electronics servicing program. The better you understand your product the more successful you can be at selling it.

Career Opportunities and Salary

Sales reps earn about the same as retail buyers, depending on their commissions. Some reps work on straight salary, but most make at least part of their income from commissions. This means that you get some of the money the customer pays. Many reps prefer a combination of salary and commission. The salary gives them a base they can depend on; the commissions are like bonuses for working hard. If your company expects you to work on straight commission and does not pay you any salary, your income may vary too much for you to feel secure.

Browse through the job placement ads in the newspaper and you will see that jobs for sales reps are plentiful. If you are willing to work hard, you should find good opportunities in this field.

TRAVEL AGENT

When someone asks you what you want to do for a living, do you say, "Travel around the world"? If you enjoy traveling and have an inclination toward sales and marketing, you may want to combine these two interests and take a job as a travel agent.

Travel agents help people plan vacations. They book airline reservations, reserve hotel rooms, and suggest tours and special attractions that they believe are worth seeing. A travel agent listens to the customer's expectations for a vacation and tries to find the right vacation package for that person.

As a fringe benefit, travel agents often have money-saving opportunities to travel, so that when they return from a trip, they can recommend it to their clients. But you will need to do more than talk about traveling if you want to be a successful travel agent. You have to be well organized and thorough about completing paperwork. Your customers will want all the connections for their vacations to go smoothly.

Education and Training

You can start preparing for this job in high school. Take classes in geography, foreign language, and computers. Although some travel agents take courses offered by junior colleges and technical schools, many work their way into travel agent positions through related entry-level jobs. When you graduate from high school, you can get a job as a receptionist in a travel agency, for example, which will help you learn the business. You may also gain valuable experience by working as a reservation clerk for an airline. Jobs such as this will help you work your way into a job as a travel agent.

Career Opportunities and Salary

Travel agents generally earn less than buyers or sales reps. Many travel agents work on commission, so salary depends on the number and cost of the trips arranged.

You will have a good chance of finding a job as a travel agent. Openings are expected to increase in the next decade.

FOR FURTHER READING

Chronicle Occupational Briefs. Moravia, N.Y.: Chronicle Guidance, 1987.

Grant, Edgar. *Exploring Careers in the Travel Industry.* New York: Rosen, 1984.

Haas, Kenneth. *Opportunities in Sales and Marketing Careers.* Chicago: National Textbook, 1980.

Hecker, Daniel, and Murphy, Ludmilla. "Retail Trade: Millions of Jobs, No Experience Necessary." *Occupational Outlook Quarterly,* Summer 1985, pp. 13–19.

Hopke, William E., ed. *The Encyclopedia of Careers and Vocational Guidance, VIII.* Chicago: Ferguson, 1984.

U.S. Dept. of Labor, Bureau of Labor Statistics. *Occupational Outlook Handbook,* 1986–7.

4

HEALTH

Dave enjoys helping people. He says the best thing about his job is the satisfaction he feels when he can make people more comfortable.

Dave works in a nursing home, caring for elderly people who are ill or disabled. He prepares and gives medication according to doctors' directions. He also keeps accurate medical records and tells the doctor about any changes he observes in his patients.

Dave started on a nursing career in the navy, where he trained for sixteen weeks to become a military corpsman. When he finished his training, he assumed many of the same duties as those of a civilian nurse.

After five and a half years, Dave left the navy and reentered civilian life. But he knew he still wanted to work as a nurse. So Dave attended a technical institute and earned an associate degree in nursing.

Nursing is a challenging job, but Dave says he gets a lot of positive feedback from his patients. They appreciate his concern and welcome his help.

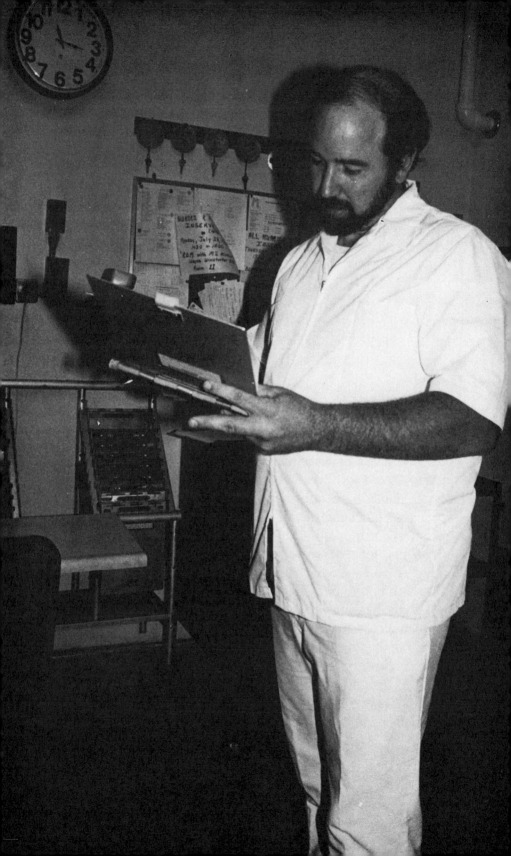

The health field is a fast-growing industry. Jobs in health occupations include physical therapists, nurses, and medical transcribers. Although we usually think of doctors when we think of the health field, doctors need many different workers on their support staff.

One reason for the increasing number of jobs in the health field is the increasing average life expectancies of our population. Another reason is the advances that have been made in medical technology. Complicated new procedures require larger support staffs and have created new jobs such as perfusionist (a technician who operates a circulatory machine during open-heart surgery) and orthotist (a technician who fits artificial legs and arms).

Traditional health care jobs also will be in demand. More openings for nurses, for example, will be available in the next ten years. In fact, there is now an acute nursing shortage in hospitals. The number of jobs for physical therapists, medical insurance clerks, occupational therapists, and physical therapy assistants is expected to double between now and 1995.

Although the health field will employ many workers in the next decade, you may find some drawbacks to jobs in this area. Health-care workers often work irregular hours since care for ill and injured patients must be available around the clock. Although salaries in this field are improving, there is often a big difference between the salaries paid to doctors and the salaries earned by nurses and health-care technicians. Traditionally, too, support jobs in

One of Dave's duties as a nurse is to keep accurate records.

health care have been held by women. Recently, however, more men have moved into nursing and health technician jobs.

In spite of the drawbacks in the health-care field, the jobs continue to give workers the special satisfaction of helping others. And the increased demands placed on the field from an aging population and technological advances make these jobs even more challenging.

The following section describes a few of the jobs in the health-care field. You can get more information about jobs in this field from a counselor at your high school or vocational school.

BIOMEDICAL EQUIPMENT TECHNICIAN

- Works well under pressure
- Has a special interest in electronics
- Likes to help people who are ill or hurt

If these qualities describe you, you may enjoy the job of a biomedical equipment technician.

Biomedical equipment technicians service health care machines such as kidney dialysis and heart-lung machines. Technicians who work in hospitals may set up new machinery, run routine tests to see that the machines are working right, and repair broken equipment. They have to work well under pressure because a patient's life may depend on how fast and accurately they can repair a life support system.

Technicians also need to know how to talk with people. They may show doctors and other hospital staff how to operate equipment.

Biomedical equipment technicians also work in places other than hospitals. For example, they may work for manufacturers of medical equipment or in laboratories testing new equipment.

If you take a job as a biomedical equipment technician, be prepared to continue to learn new information. This fast-paced, high-tech career is continually changing.

Education and Training

Study chemistry, physics, and math while you are in high school. You can then earn an associate degree in biomedical equipment technology. As part of your education, you will have on-the-job training in a hospital or in a medical center. Here you will learn to apply your classroom learning to actual experiences.

Some people who have associate degrees in electronics or instrumentation technology also find jobs in the medical field.

Career Opportunities

After you have worked a few years as a biomedical equipment technician, you can take a test to get a special license. If you pass this test you will be able to advance in your field.

With hospital experience, you can earn a promotion to supervisor. Some technicians return to school to earn a bachelor's degree in biomedical engineering. Another area open to biomedical equipment technicians who have good communication skills is sales. This is a good area for someone interested in electronics who also likes to work with people. You would sell biomedical equipment to hospitals, laboratories, clinics, and so on.

EMERGENCY MEDICAL TECHNICIAN

Would you like to make a career of helping people in danger? If you are a strong, healthy person and think you could act efficiently and effectively in emergency situations, you rmay find a career as an EMT—emergency medical technician—challenging.

Emergency medical technicians provide first aid to ill or injured people. They may give CPR (cardiopulmonary resuscitation) to a heart attack victim or tend to an auto accident victim in shock. Although they are often the first trained people to arrive on the scene, EMTs may work closely with a doctor who relays instructions to them over a shortwave radio.

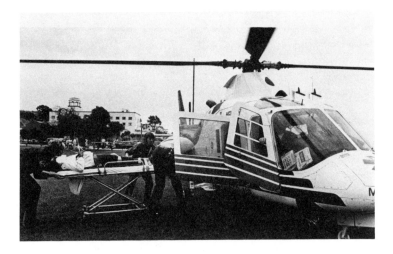

Emergency medical technicians are often the first trained medical personnel to attend to sick or injured people who need emergency treatment.

The first concern of the EMT is to decide how badly the person is hurt and to stabilize the patient's condition. They then usually go with the patient to a hospital or treatment center, where a doctor takes over the care of the patient.

EMTs work for police or fire departments, hospitals, and medical centers. They put in long hours, sometimes more than fifty hours a week. You can expect to work weekends, nights, and holidays if you choose this job. Although the work can be stressful, it is also greatly rewarding.

Education and Training

You can start training for a career as an emergency medical technician while you are in high school. Take classes in health and science as well as driver's education, because you may need to drive an ambulance or other rescue vehicle to the scene of the accident. You will also need to know how to talk to people under stress. English classes can help you improve your communication skills.

There are several ways to train specifically for a job as an emergency medical technician. One way is to join the armed forces and train as a medic. Another way is to enroll in a basic training program that is taught in hospitals and police departments. This course includes 100 hours of training in emergency first aid. You will learn how to control bleeding, open blocked airways, and handle patients. When you complete this course you can be certified as an emergency medical technician.

When you have completed your training, you will have to take a licensing test from the National Registry of Emergency Medical Technicians. When you pass the written and practical parts of the test, you will earn the classification

Registered EMT—Ambulance. This registration must be renewed every two years.

Career Opportunities and Salary

Many city fire departments call on volunteer EMTs to staff their rescue vehicles. From your job as a volunteer, you can work your way into a permanent paid position. EMTs earn more with experience and certification as an EMT—Paramedic. Certification requires an additional 600 to 1,000 hours of training.

Although you may need to start your career as a volunteer, you will have a good chance of finding a job as an EMT.

DENTAL HYGIENIST

Dental hygienists clean teeth, apply fluoride treatments, and take dental X-rays. They also teach patients how to care for their teeth by showing them how to brush and floss and describe the way that smoking or chewing tobacco affects the mouth. Dental hygienists are often asked to give talks to schoolchildren about how to take care of their teeth.

Because patients in dental offices are often fearful, a hygienist needs a friendly, cheerful manner to help the patients relax. If you are good with your hands, outgoing, personable, and easygoing, being a dental hygienist may be right for you.

Dental hygienists work in dental offices, but they often work independently. Unlike a dental assistant, who works directly with the dentist, hygienists work alone. They schedule their own appointments and build their own practice. They often work in an office with several dentists. In

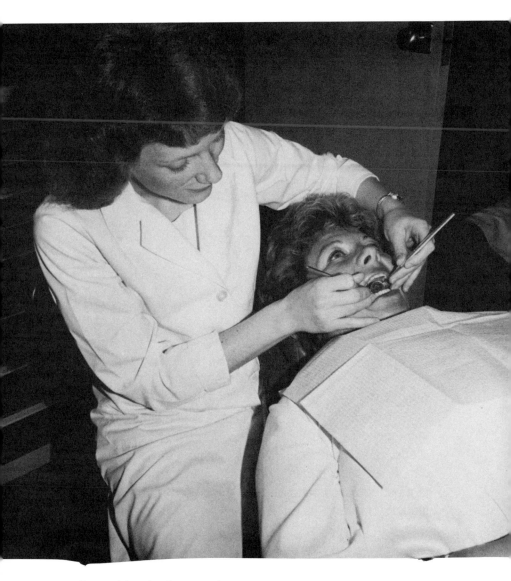

Dental hygienists work on a
one-to-one basis with their
patients, cleaning their teeth and
offering advice on dental care.

some cases they are employed by the dentist; in other cases they work for a commission based on how many patients they see each week. To earn a living in this field, you may need to work for two or more dental offices, because one office may not have enough work to keep you busy full time.

Education and Training

To prepare for this field, take classes in health, speech, and science while in high school. You will need these courses to earn an associate degree from an approved technical institute or junior college. Dental hygienists must be licensed. To receive a license as a dental hygienist you must graduate from an approved program and pass a standard test. The test includes both a written part and a clinical part, in which you show how well you can apply your knowledge of actual office experience.

In school, dental hygienists study nutrition, gum disease, and chemistry. They learn how to use dental tools, polish teeth, and talk with patients.

The armed forces offer classes in dental hygiene, but this instruction usually is not enough for you to pass the licensing exam needed to work in private practice. You can, however, get credit for your armed forces experience at most approved schools. This credit usually shortens your training time and helps you earn an associate degree in less than two years.

Career Opportunities

No one is sure how many jobs there will be for dental hygienists in the next decade, but right now, career opportunities look good in this field.

RADIOLOGIC TECHNOLOGIST

Are you looking for a job in a high-tech field? Would you like a job that combines the most modern technological advances with old-fashioned concern for people? If this combination appeals to you, you might enjoy the job of radiologic technologist.

A radiologic technologist works with radiation in various forms. There are two main types of work. Diagnostic "rad techs" may take X-rays, ultrasounds, or other pictures of the internal organs. Therapeutic "rad techs" use radiation to treat patients.

Radiologic technologists usually work in hospitals. They should be sympathetic, caring people because they often work with people who are very ill or dying.

Radiologic technologists should be aware of the health risks to themselves. Because they are working with radiation, they need to use lead aprons and partitions that shield them from exposure to radiation. While on the job you may be expected to wear a device that records radiation levels to make sure your work area stays within safe limits. Most aspects of work in this field are regulated by the federal government, so the exposure hazards are minimal.

Education and Training

You can train for this job at hospitals, at technical institutes, and in the armed services. Although training programs vary, most last about two years. Often hospitals work in cooperation with technical institutes to provide classroom information with on-the-job experience. In some states you will need a license to practice.

When choosing a school, make sure it is approved by the Committee on Allied Health Education and Accreditation. This committee sets standards for the courses that the schools offer. Most hospitals require that their employees are graduated only from certified schools.

Career Opportunities and Salary

Jobs are quite easy to find in this field, with experienced technicians specializing in fields such as ultrasound and nuclear medicine drawing the highest salaries. Radiologic technology is a rapidly expanding field because we continue to find new ways to use radiation in the treatment and diagnosis of disease.

NURSE

- Accepts responsibility
- Sympathizes with people when they are hurt or ill
- Shows good judgment

Nurses hold highly responsible jobs, and it is important for them to have these qualities.

Most nurses work in hospitals. They follow doctors' directions in caring for people who are ill or recovering from operations. They give medicine, record blood pressure and other important information, and help to cheer up patients who are sad or depressed. They also talk to the patient's family members, answering their questions and giving them advice about how to care for the patient at home.

Although nursing is a personally rewarding job, it is also very demanding, especially in hospitals. Nurses must be able to work under pressure and in difficult situations. They must be able to accept death. Nurses also often work

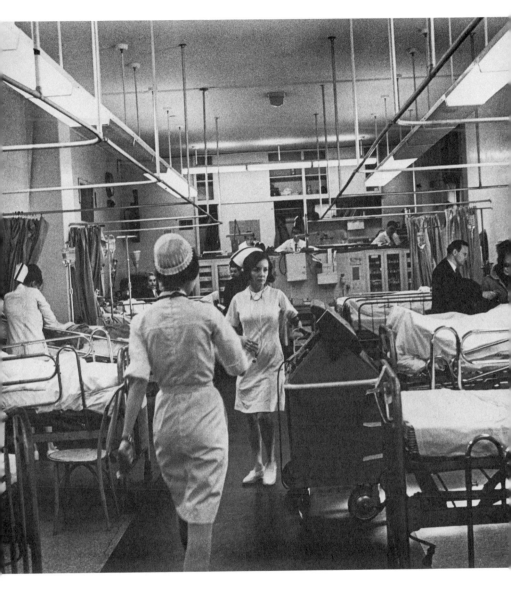

Nurses at work in a ward at New York City's Bellevue Hospital.

irregular hours. They may work rotating shifts, weekends, and holidays.

Some nurses work in private homes caring for home-bound patients or in nursing homes caring for the elderly. Some nurses also work for schools and industries. They treat patients who have had minor accidents and teach students and employees how to keep well.

Nurses usually specialize. They may work in surgery, pediatrics, or in the emergency room, for example.

Education and Training

You will need a license to work as a nurse. To get this license you must have a degree in nursing and pass a national examination given by the state in which you want to work.

Although many nurses have bachelor's degrees from four-year schools, you do not need a four-year degree to qualify for the exam. In fact, almost 70 percent of all nurses have one-year diplomas or two-year associate degrees from junior colleges or technical schools.

In these programs you will study biology, anatomy, and nutrition. You will use what you learn in class in actual nursing situations. Nursing programs include clinical train-ing during which students work in a hospital or clinic envi-ronment. Their classroom instructors supervise their work on the job. Nursing students also take some English and speech classes to improve their ability to write reports and talk with patients and other hospital staff.

Career Opportunities and Salary

Nurses with associate degrees can continue their educa-tion by earning a bachelor's degree. This increases their chances for promotion and higher salaries. Nurses with associate degrees may move up to supervisory positions in a nursing home but need a four-year degree to advance to head nurse or supervisor in a hospital.

Many women who used to become nurses are now either unwilling to work under hospital conditions or are going into more financially rewarding careers. That is one reason there is a serious shortage of trained nurses, especially in hospitals. Opportunities are plentiful in the field, and some hospitals have now upgraded the role—and salaries—of their nurses.

FOR FURTHER READING

Braddock, Douglas. "Careers in the New Technologies: Biotechnology." *Occupational Outlook Quarterly,* Summer 1985, pp. 5–11.

Chronicle Occupational Briefs. Moravia, N.Y.: Chronicle Guidance, 1987.

Downs, Florence, and Brooten, Dorothy. *New Careers in Nursing.* New York: Arco, 1983.

Frederickson, Keville. *Opportunities in Nursing.* Chicago: National Textbook, 1983.

Heron, Jackie. *Exploring Careers.* New York: Rosen, 1986.

Hopke, William E., ed. *The Encyclopedia of Careers and Vocational Guidance, VIII.* Chicago: Ferguson, 1984.

Kacen, Alex. *Opportunities in Paramedical Careers.* Chicago: National Textbook, 1983.

Kahl, Anne, and Clerk, Donald E. "Health: Crossroads Over the Horizon?" *Occupational Outlook Quarterly,* Summer 1985, pp. 5–11.

Marten, Gail M. "Medical Technology of the 1980s: Giving Birth to New Health Careers." *Occupational Outlook Quarterly,* Winter 1983, pp. 3–14.

Seide, Diane. *Careers in Health Services.* New York: Lodestar Books, 1982.

U.S. Dept. of Labor, Bureau of Labor Statistics. *Occupational Outlook Handbook,* 1986–7.

5

OFFICES AND BUSINESSES

"Good morning," Rhonda says when she answers the phone. "This is Rhonda. How can I help you?"

It seems to Rhonda that the phone starts ringing the minute she walks into her office. As a secretary, one of her most important jobs is communicating on the telephone. That's why, even when she is rushed, Rhonda tries to answer the phone pleasantly.

Rhonda is also skilled at word processing. Recently, her office added a computer and Rhonda took a class in word processing. Now she uses the word processor for her office reports and letters.

Rhonda's job has a lot of variety. She schedules appointments, types letters, and answers the phone. She greets people when they come into the office and answers questions about office routine.

As the number of service industries increases, so does the demand for support services in the business sector. A greater number of lawyers or insurance agents, for example, increases the need for the secretaries and receptionists who work for them.

The growing automation of offices as well as factories has resulted in additional business career openings for people who can work with computers. Computer operators and systems analysts, for example, will be in demand in the future. Altogether, about 19 million people now have jobs in support services to businesses.

Many opportunities are available to you in the business world. Business occupations include jobs in banks and offices. You may find an entry-level job as a receptionist or bank teller or computer operator. Most people in business work regular hours at fairly predictable jobs. This is one of the advantages of a job in this area. Another advantage is that there is a lot of room for career advancement in this field. You may take a job as a secretary and work your way up to an assistant-level position with more responsibility and better pay. This kind of advancement is available to motivated employees in business.

In the following sections we look at a few of the opportunities in business and office occupations.

SECRETARY

Are you a good planner? Do you do well in spelling tests? Do your friends ask you to check their themes for correct punctuation and grammar? If so, you may want to consider becoming a secretary.

Secretaries type letters, make appointments, and file information. Their bosses depend on them to arrange schedules and keep the office work flowing efficiently.

Secretaries may specialize in a particular type of work. For example, legal secretaries work for lawyers. They prepare legal documents and help with research. A medical secretary transcribes medical reports and files medical records. To do the job right, the medical secretary must be familiar with medical terms and the legal secretary must understand legal jargon.

Although a secretary's work can be varied and interesting, it can also be frustrating. As a secretary, you will need to know how to cope with interruption. Secretaries must stop typing letters to answer the phone. They must interrupt their work to answer questions from various people. Such interruptions are part of a secretary's workday.

Education and Training

If you have taken typing or word processing and office skills classes in high school you will qualify for many secretarial jobs. But if you want to specialize in medical or legal work, for example, you will probably need an associate degree from a technical school or junior college.

Secretaries should also have good communication skills. They should be able to write business letters according to their boss's suggestions and answer the phone politely. Secretaries should also know how to listen and how to relate to people.

As offices automate, training on a word processor is becoming increasingly important to a secretary. Many secretaries use a word processor for at least some of their office work.

If you choose to be a secretary, you may need to take refresher courses regularly. Office machinery, such as word processors and computers, changes rapidly and secretaries must keep up with these changes to organize their work efficiently. Your employer will often pay for the classes you take to update your skills.

Career Opportunities and Salary

Salaries vary widely, depending on the company, type of business, responsibilities, and region of the country. If you do a good job as a secretary, you may be able to move into other jobs in the company. Some people in midmanagement positions started their careers as secretaries.

On the other hand, secretarial positions also lend themselves to temporary or part-time work, if this fits your life-style. Secretaries, for example, may be employed in permanent part-time positions in which they work an average of twenty hours a week.

When you train for a secretarial position, you have a good chance of finding steady work. This field is one of the largest of any in the United States.

LEGAL ASSISTANT

Do you enjoy looking up information for a report to your class? Can you organize your thoughts logically? If you do well on research assignments in school, you might do well as a legal assistant.

Legal assistants, also called paralegals, work closely with lawyers to prepare for court cases. They research laws and gather information pertaining to each case. Then they

An office such as this,
at the Crow Indian tribal
offices in Montana,
employs a number of people
who do secretarial duties.

put all this background information into a written report that the attorney may use to prepare the case for court. Paralegals may also prepare documents to be used in court and keep files of each case.

Legal assistants must think logically and be able to organize information. They must research thoroughly so all parts of the problem are covered. They must also be able to clearly write down the facts so the lawyer understands what they have learned. Paralegals are a little like detectives. They find information to help solve problems. Since a lot of their research is done through computers, computer skills are also helpful.

Most legal assistants work for private law offices, but they may also work in banks, insurance companies, or real estate agencies.

Although the job pays quite well and is usually interesting, paralegals often work long hours and are under pressure to meet deadlines. They must be careful to do a thorough job even when they need to hurry.

Education and Training

Although some employers train legal assistants on the job, most lawyers prefer to hire graduates of a training program. Vocational schools and community colleges offer two-year legal assistant programs. These programs train people in research and technical writing skills. They offer courses in legal terms and computer skills. An internship in a legal office is usually part of the training program.

Another way to qualify for a job as a legal assistant is to earn an associate degree as a legal secretary and work your way into a paralegal position.

Legal assistant is a fairly new occupation, so requirements for the job vary. Although you do not need a license to be hired as a legal assistant, a certificate is helpful in finding a job. When you pass a two-day exam from the National Association of Legal Assistants, you have earned the title of Certified Legal Assistant.

Career Opportunities and Salary

You will have a good chance of finding a job as a paralegal. Paralegals are often hired to help keep legal costs down, and so, with today's high legal costs, paralegals are much in demand.

Since lawyers can earn much more than paralegals, it is not uncommon for a person who is a legal assistant to use his or her job as a stepping-stone to becoming a lawyer. After a few years working as a paralegal for a lawyer, paralegals often return to school to earn a law degree.

COMPUTER OPERATOR

A computer operator follows instructions written by computer programmers to enter and retrieve data. If you choose this job, you will locate specific information and run entire programs for other office personnel.

Computer operators work in insurance offices and hospitals. They find jobs in state governments and in private industries. When a workplace, such as a hospital, uses its computers around the clock, computer operators work evening shifts. As the work world increases its dependence on computers, computer operators will be needed in most workplaces. You can choose an area that interests you and apply your computer skills to that field.

Computer use is widespread in offices.

Education and Training

Although you may learn the necessary skills for this job in high school or in adult-education courses, you should consider earning an associate degree in data processing from a community college or technical school. Employers often prefer applicants for computer jobs to have some training beyond high school. You may also choose the military as a way to get training for a job as a computer operator.

Even if you have a degree, you should expect to participate in an on-the-job training program. Computer systems and procedures vary from office to office, and you will need time to get used to a new system.

In school, computer operators study computer languages, programming, and computer operations. They also may take classes in accounting and technical writing.

Career Opportunities

The Bureau of Labor Statistics lists computer operator as one of the faster-growing occupations for the next decade.

Although jobs are plentiful, the chances for advancement are limited because the training is quite specialized. You may move up to supervisor of a data processing department, but you will need additional training to qualify for other positions.

BANK TELLER

Do you like to meet people? Are your arithmetic skills first-rate? If so, you may enjoy being a bank teller.

A bank teller greets customers and helps them with their banking needs. Tellers cash checks, make deposits, and record loan payments. Bank tellers must work very carefully. They are instructed to ask for the customer's identification before cashing a check. A driver's licence or credit card helps the teller make sure that the person cashing the check is actually the one to whom the check is written.

Bank tellers must also be accurate. They make sure that loan payments and savings deposits are entered in the right account. They also take care to count out the exact amount when cashing a check. Every penny must be accounted for at the end of the day.

Tellers use adding machines and computers to help them in their work. They call up customer accounts on computer terminals and total deposits and withdrawals on adding machines.

Sometimes people say, "I'd like to work in a bank. They have short working days." You have probably heard people say, "She has banker's hours," when they mean she has an easy workday.

But bank employees work more hours than people think. Bank tellers arrive before the bank opens. They pick up their cash drawer from a supervisor and count the money in the drawer. At the end of the day they stay after the bank has closed to count the money in their cash drawer again, and to balance their accounts.

Bank tellers help customers with their banking. They cash checks, make deposits, and record loan payments, among other duties.

Tellers may also work evenings and weekends. You should be prepared to work a varied schedule to meet the customer's needs.

Education and Training

Most bank tellers have high school diplomas, but banks may hire you for this position even if you have not graduated from high school. Banks are willing to hire people with little experience because most banks train their own tellers.

Career Opportunities

Bank teller is usually an entry-level position. If you do well, you can advance to the position of head teller or customer service representative. By taking advantage of classes offered by the bank in which you work, or through the American Institute of Banking, you can prepare for a managerial job in a bank or qualify for a promotion to bank officer.

FOR FURTHER READING

Bailey, David, and Castors, Laura. *Careers in Computers.* New York: Messner, 1985.

Berkey, Rachel Lane. *New Career Opportunities in the Paralegal Profession.* New York: Arco, 1983.

Brechner, Irv. *Getting into Computers: A Career Guide to Today's New Field.* New York: Ballantine, 1983.

Chronicle Occupational Briefs. Moravia, N.Y.: Chronicle Guidance, 1987.

Consumer Guide Publicatons International Ltd. *Computer Careers: Where the Jobs Are and How to Get Them.* New York: Ballantine, 1984.

Ettinger, Blanche, and Popham, Estelle. *Opportunities in Office Occupations.* Chicago: National Textbook, 1982.

——. *Opportunities in Secretarial Careers.* Chicago: National Textbook, 1984.

Ferres, Theodore, N., ed. *Computer Operator.* St. Paul, Minn.: Changing Times, 1980.

Fins, Alice. *Opportunities in a Paralegal Career.* Chicago: National Textbook, 1984.

Hopke, William E., ed. *The Encyclopedia of Careers and Vocational Guidance, VIII.* Chicago: Ferguson, 1984.

Parades, Adrian A. *Opportunities in Banking.* Chicago: National Textbook, 1986.

Prendergast, Lesley J. *Secretary to Paralegal: A Career Manual and Guide.* Englewood Cliffs, N.J.: Institute of Business Planning, 1984.

Spencer, Jean W. *Exploring Careers in the Electronic Office.* New York: Rosen, 1985.

U.S. Dept of Labor, Bureau of Labor Statistics. *Occupational Outlook Handbook,* 1986–7.

6

INDUSTRY

"This is an expanding field," Ron says about his job as an instrumentation technician. "It's a good job for stable, long-term employment." That's one of the reasons Ron chose a career as an instrument technician. Another reason is because he finds the job interesting and challenging.

Ron works for a company that manufactures pollution control systems. He calibrates instrument panels and checks to make sure the equipment is running properly.

Although Ron does most of his work at his home plant, he says instrument technicians must be prepared to travel. They often go to the job site and set up equipment for the customer. When Ron is working on a start-up, he may put in long hours to get the system running properly.

Ron has worked as an instrument technician for eleven years, and during that time his job has taken many interesting turns. For example, now he writes manuals telling people how to operate the equipment he calibrates.

Would you like a factory job like Ron's after you graduate from high school? Maybe, even though you want to

Instrumentation technicians like Ron test and adjust equipment.

work in a factory, you are searching for other kinds of work because you have been told there won't be any factory jobs in the future.

True, the number of factory jobs has declined in the last five years. In the 1970s manufacturing accounted for 33 percent of all jobs. In the future only about 7 percent of us will work in factories.

Factory jobs are changing, too. In the past many jobs in manufacturing were entry-level jobs that required minimal skills. Today most factory jobs require some training. If you plan to work in a factory, you will need some background in electronics or computers. Most factory workers in the future will use computerized equipment to do their work.

You should also probably think of robots as co-workers. By 1990 as many as 100,000 robots may be part of the manufacturing process. Many available factory jobs will be in robot supervision, programming, and repair.

You will probably need training beyond high school. You should enroll in a one- or two-year industrial program offered at vocational schools. Some of the jobs you can train for are robotics technician, instrumentation technician, and numerical-control machine-tool operator.

Some factory workers can still get jobs without special training. They begin as a shop's helper and work their way into skilled positions. But to work their way into skilled positions, they need to acquire technical skills somewhere along the way. Some industries offer on-the-job training; others send their employees to vocational schools to receive specialized training.

You should be prepared to compete for the limited number of factory jobs available. Your best means of competition is specialized training in one or more phases of manufacturing. In the future, factory workers will need to be increasingly better educated.

The following sections provide descriptions of a few industrial jobs.

NUMERICAL-CONTROL
MACHINE-TOOL OPERATOR

Would you like to get a high-paying factory job when you graduate from high school? If that career route appeals to you, you should consider a job as a numerical-control machine-tool operator.

Machine-tool operators shape metal parts by cutting or drilling them on a machine. They make parts for airplanes, automobiles, stoves, and bicycles. A machine-tool operator cuts each of the parts needed for a product from sheet metal.

Numerical control (NC) means that the cutting machine is run by a computer. In the past, machine-tool operators guided the metal through the machine by hand. Today they put the metal into the machine. Then they punch a code into a computer and the machine shapes the metal according to instructions it gets from the computer. Some NC operators also write the instructions—the programs—that tell the machine what to do. Operators may work on one machine or on several machines in their work area.

If you choose this job, be prepared to repeat one or two tasks many times during the day. This repetition is one of the drawbacks some people find in this job.

Education and Training

Most NC operators start in a factory as a shop's helper doing a variety of tasks. From there, they may get a job as a machine-tool operator and eventually move up to a position as operator of an NC machine. Most NC machine-tool operators do not have vocational school training, but they may have special on-the-job training. Good work habits, reliability, and the ability to follow directions are necessary skills in this occupation.

Career Opportunities

As factories automate, the number of positions for NC operators will increase. Job opportunities will be good in this field in the next decade.

You may work your way up to unit supervisor or into a job as a tool programmer, the person who writes the programs the operator uses to run the machines.

Many jobs for machine-tool operators, including punch press operator, lathe operator, and milling operator, are available. But the NC machine-tool operator will probably have the best chance of finding factory work in the future. The demand will be greatest for workers who can use computers to manufacture parts.

CAD OPERATOR

CAD is short for computer-aided design, and a CAD operator uses a computer to do a drafter's job. The CAD operator uses a light-pen and a keyboard to make drawings instead of the ruler, pen, and ink used by other drafters. Errors are erased at the touch of a finger and new lines are drawn just as quickly. Some computers even display drawings in "three dimensions" so the drafter can see how the product will look when it is put together.

CAD systems help drafters make drawings more quickly, and drafters with computer skills are in demand. Except for knowing how to use a computer, a CAD operator's skills are those of any other drafter. It may, however, take a while for you to transfer your drafting skills to a computer. Most manufacturers say that it takes four to six months to become as good on the computer as on the drawing board.

If you are interested in this job you should be able to do accurate drawings and visualize complicated diagrams and three-dimensional objects. You should also be able to work as a team member. Drafters are the middle people between engineers and manufacturers. A drafter takes an

When Lance started drafting ten years ago, he used paper and pencil to make his drawings. Today he uses a computer.

engineer's rough sketch and turns it into a completed design. The manufacturer uses that design to produce the product. Although you will find that the computer makes your work easier, CAD operators may experience eye strain and must take regular breaks from the computer.

Education and Training

You can begin training for a job as a CAD operator in high school with classes in mechanical drawing and mathematics.

After high school you can enroll in a one- or two-year vocational school program. These programs stress traditional drafting skills using a computer. Remember, the computer is just a tool you use for drafting. You do not need to know how to program or service the computer to use it in your drafting work.

Some people also train as CAD operators on the job. For those who have good drafting skills a three- to four-week course in the use of the computer is enough training. Apprenticeship programs and training during military service are other ways you can prepare for this occupation.

Career Opportunities

Although computer-aided design is used in only about 10 percent of the industries that employ drafters, it is a growing field. Nearly 350,000 jobs are expected by 1995.

ROBOTICS TECHNICIAN

Thousands of robots operate in factories across the United States. These robots must be serviced and repaired. New robots must be installed to meet the growing demand for automation in our factories. If you are interested in working with computerized equipment, you may want to train for a job as a robotics technician.

When technicians install a robot, they program it to do a specific task such as welding and cutting. They make sure the robot is doing that task correctly and consistently. Some of the jobs that robots are trained to do are dangerous; therefore, robotic technicians have to take care when setting up these robots.

When a robot is installed, technicians train factory workers, called robot attendants, to supervise the robot's operation. They tell these attendants how the robot should work and show them how to spot robots that do not work properly.

Good communication skills will help you succeed as a robotics technician. You must know how to listen to an attendant describing what's wrong with a robot. You must be able to teach an attendant to tend a robot efficiently.

Robotics technicians may work for a large factory or for a robot manufacturer. If you work for a manufacturer you will travel from factory to factory installing and servicing robots purchased from your company.

Education and Training

You can begin training for this job in high school. Take classes in speech, computer programming, and electronics.

After high school, you can go to a vocational school to take a two-year program in electromechanical technology in which you learn to repair electronic equipment. You can also take a one-year program in robotics repair. This is such a new field that the courses to train robotics technicians are just beginning to develop. You should tell the vocational school counselor what you want to do and let that person suggest a training program for you. The program you choose should include classes in computer repair and programming and electronics technology.

Career Opportunities

Although job opportunities are limited in this field now, 200,000 are expected to open up by 1995 as more factories automate.

Robotics technicians also have a good chance to move up in their field. With additional education, they may move into jobs as trainers of other robotics technicians or as supervisors of servicing departments.

WELDER

Can you concentrate on detailed work for long periods of time? Do you have good eye-hand coordination? If you do and you want work in a factory, you may want to consider the job of welder.

Welders use heat to join metal parts. Welding is used to connect parts during the manufacture of cars, ships, and airplanes, for example.

Although some welding is routine and may even be handled by a robot, other types of welding require specialized skills. Skilled welders may work in several areas, including maintenance welding and pressure vessel welding. Maintenance welders fix broken pipes, tools, and other machinery. They find the damaged area and use the right

tools to repair it. Pressure vessel welders follow blueprints to join parts for nuclear reactors and submarines.

Welding can be a hazardous job. Welders wear helmets, goggles, and special shoes to protect them against burns and injuries. Welders work in a variety of places, including aircraft factories. They also go into the field when they work on bridges and utility pipelines, for example.

Education and Training

You can learn to be a welder in a one-year diploma course offered by technical schools and community colleges. Your high school may even have a welding program. In these programs you will study mathematics and blueprint reading as well as arc and gas welding.

Some welders don't go to vocational school. They learn to weld through on-the-job training. They start with simple welds and progress to advanced projects that require specialized skills.

The military also offers training in welding, and skills learned in the armed forces can be transferred to civilian industries.

You should prepare now if you plan to enter a welding program after you graduate from high school. You should take courses in math, drafting, and physics while you are in high school.

When this student actually begins to weld, she will lower her face mask to protect her face and eyes.

Career Opportunities

Although the number of routine welding jobs may decrease as robots take over more of these tasks, skilled welders should find good career opportunities in the next decade.

If you want to work as a welder, plan to get specialized training so you can work in the skilled areas in which robots are not used.

INSTRUMENTATION TECHNICIAN

If you have a "mind for details" and like to work at something until you have it perfect, you may be suited for a job as an instrumentation technician.

Instrument technicians make sure that factory equipment is running accurately. They adjust gauges that control pressure, temperature, and motion in industrial machinery. For example, they may work in nuclear power plants making sure the safety instruments are in top shape. Instrument technicians may install equipment, repair instruments, or do periodic checks on machines to make sure they are running properly. They adjust the gauges so that the machines run efficiently.

Instrumentation technicians may work in factories, hospitals, or other places in which machinery is used. Some instrumentation technicians also help design instruments or work in laboratories testing equipment.

Education and Training

You can begin training for this job in high school by taking jobs in computer science, electronics, and math.

Most instrument technicians earn an associate degree in instrumentation technology, but you may also qualify for work in this area with a degree in electronics or mechanics. Although you should have training in electronics, you will also need some knowledge of computer technology, because many machines are computerized.

Career Opportunities

Instrumentation technology is a challenging high-tech field offering excellent chances for employment. Instrument technicians can advance to supervisory positions. The demand for instrumentation technicians increases as factories automate. In 1986 there were more job openings in this field than there were qualified people to fill them. Although all areas of the country need technicians, most of the best opportunities are in Texas and California.

FOR FURTHER READING

Career Opportunities in the Tooling and Machining Industry. National Tooling and Machining Association, 9300 Livingston Rd., Fort Washington, MD 20744.

Chronicle Occupational Briefs. Moravia, N.Y.: *Chronicle Guidance,* 1987.

Consider a Career in Welding. Lincoln Electric Company, 22801 St. Clair Ave., Cleveland, OH 44117.

Focus on Your Future. American Welding Society, P.O. Box 351040, Miami, FL 33135.

Hopke, William E., ed. *The Encyclopedia of Careers and Vocational Guidance, VIII.* Chicago: Ferguson, 1984.

Lee, Mary, and Lee, Richard. *Exploring Careers in Robotics.* New York: Rosen, 1984.

Make Your Career Choice Robotics. Robotics International of SME, One SME Drive, P.O. Box 930, Dearborn, MI 48121.

Shanahan, William F. *Guide to Apprenticeship Programs.* New York: Arco, 1983.

U.S. Dept. of Labor, Bureau of Labor Statistics. *Occupational Outlook Handbook,* 1986–7.

7

BUILDING TRADES

When Pat goes to work, she dresses in special rubber gloves, a hard hat, and steel-toed shoes. Pat is an electrician for a paper mill. She services new equipment and troubleshoots machines already in operation. She finds out what's wrong with broken-down equipment and repairs it.

Pat has worked as an electrician for six years. She started as a helper in the mill's electrical shop. She worked during the summers while she went to school. As a shop's helper, she worked with experienced electricians and learned her trade through hands-on experience.

Pat liked the work and decided to take a full-time job as an electrician. Once on the job, she knew she would need more training, so she enrolled in an apprenticeship program. While working full time, she went to school at a local technical institute one or two days a week. The time Pat spent in school was well worth the effort. Today Pat is a journeyman electrician and enjoys the challenges and variety of work her job offers.

"One of the most important things you can do to prepare for this job," Pat says, "is study math." Pat's four years of high school math helped her get through the apprenticeship program successfully. Pat stresses that studying math helps improve your logical reasoning skills, which are very important in an electrician's job.

If you want a job as an electrician, Pat recommends finding an entry-level job in the field and taking advantage of the company's training program.

Construction workers build homes, office complexes, shopping malls, and factories. They also repair and remodel buildings. In this field you may find a job as a drafter, plumber, electrician, drywaller, or carpenter.

Jobs in the building trades fluctuate with the economy. When interest rates are low and the economy is stable, construction jobs are plentiful. During a recession, however, workers in the building trades may be laid off. Some construction jobs are seasonal. Most building, for example, is done during the dry, warm times of the year. Winter snows and seasonal rains slow up business in construction. If you can live with fluctuations in the market you can earn a good income from an interesting job in construction.

Construction workers may work in a variety of locations, commuting several hours each day to and from a job site. Some construction jobs require you to join a union and others do not. However, maintenance work is needed all year round.

As an industrial electrician in a paper mill, Pat keeps large motors running smoothly.

Despite some seasonal fluctuation and dependence on a favorable economy the construction industry remains a good source of jobs.

A few jobs in this industry are described in the following pages.

ARCHITECTURAL DRAFTER

Would you like to work in an architectural firm, drawing plans for houses and shopping malls, but you do not want to take the time for four years of college just now? You could consider earning an associate degree as an architectural drafter.

Architectural drafters draw plans for houses and apartment buildings. They may work with architects in the design of the building, and then use their drafting skills to draw up the plan. Architectural drafters work for architects doing drafting and estimating. They may also find jobs building houses.

Education and Training

Start preparing for this job in high school by taking classes in mechanical drawing, blueprint reading, art, and math. After high school, go to vocational school for a one- or two-year course in architectural drafting. Study mechanical drawing, estimating, and technologies related to the housing industry. Drafters with associate degrees have the best chance of getting a job.

Career Opportunities

If you have experience using a computer to draw building plans, you will have the best chance for success in this field. Employers are most willing to hire people with computer skills.

CONSTRUCTION MACHINERY OPERATOR

Construction machinery operators help in the construction industry by clearing land and lifting heavy material. As a construction machinery operator, you might use a tower crane to raise steel girders or to lift heavy panes of glass.

Construction operators help build dams and roads. They work for mining and logging companies. They work on office buildings, hospitals, and factories.

Most construction machinery operators find a special thrill in running these powerful machines. But the work can also be noisy and hard. The constant jarring of the big machines makes operators feel tired, and driving the machines in very cold or hot weather can also be difficult.

You may also find that you must travel from job site to job site in order to keep working. One job may take you to a small town to build a dam. Another job may take you several hundred miles away to a large city to help put up a skyscraper.

The successful operator must be careful, coordinated, and able to follow directions. Operators often get directions from someone in a control tower who tells them how to steer their machinery and where to place their loads. You should also be able to follow hand signals to run your machine.

Education and Training

You can become a construction machinery operator by working your way up from entry-level jobs in the construc-

tion business. For example, you can get a job helping the operator keep the big machines in working order. These helpers, called "oilers," make sure that the equipment is filled with fuel and ready to go. Gradually, oilers learn how to repair and operate the machines. When they have enough experience, they can move into jobs as construction machine operators. Although supervisors in the construction business recommend the industry's apprenticeship program, most operators seem to learn their trade from on-the-job experience.

You can learn to be a construction machinery operator through a three-year apprenticeship. This program combines schooling with on-the-job training. In school, apprentices study hydraulics, engine operation, and first aid. On the job they learn how to operate the heavy equipment and keep it in working order.

Career Opportunities and Salary

If you train as an operator, you will have a good chance of getting a job, and you will earn a good salary. As is true of other construction workers, operators may be laid off when building is slow. Construction machinery operators also do not have much chance for advancement. Only a few become supervisors.

Construction machinery operators work on a variety of projects, including roads and dams.

SURVEYOR

- Good in math
- Pays attention to details
- Can visualize distances and sizes
- Works well in a group.

These are some things a successful surveyor does well.

Surveyors map out land boundaries. They write legal descriptions of land and gather information to use in drawing maps and charts. When a city wants to build a road, the town council hires a surveyor to map out the route of the road. A farmer who wants to put up a fence may hire a surveyor to find the boundaries of the farm. A contractor who wants to divide a field into building lots may hire a surveyor to mark the boundaries.

Surveyors usually work in groups called survey parties. They use delicate instruments to measure angles and distances. Surveyors spend a lot of time outdoors. Often they must walk through woods and swamps and over hills. Usually they must pack heavy equipment on their backs.

Surveyors also spend a lot of time in an office. After they have plotted the land boundaries outdoors, they return to the office to draw maps and write up the information they have gathered. Some people think a surveyor's job is just the right combination of indoor and outdoor work.

Education and Training

You can train to be a surveyor in a variety of ways. One way is to enroll in a surveying program at a junior college or technical institute. These courses usually last one or two years.

Surveyors work in all kinds of settings.

You can also learn this trade from on-the-job training. After graduation from high school you can join a survey crew and learn how to use and care for the various surveying instruments. Gradually you can work your way up to more challenging jobs.

Career Opportunities and Salary

You will need dedication to your job to reach career heights as a surveyor. Pay is fairly low for high school graduates but higher if you have an associate degree from a technical school or junior college.

To reach the top-paying jobs in this field, you must be licensed as a land surveyor. Every state in the United States requires this licensing. Licensing requirements vary, but you may need as many as five to twelve years' experience to meet the requirements. Once you are licensed, your income will be good. Licensed surveyors earn about double the pay of unlicensed ones.

Opportunities for surveyors are expected to increase in the next ten years.

PLUMBER

Plumbers install the pipe systems that carry fresh water to buildings and waste water away. Plumbers may work in new-home construction installing copper or plastic piping

Dan learned the plumbing business through an apprenticeship program. Today he owns his own business.

and hooking it up to sinks, toilets, bathtubs, and dishwashers. They may also work with the large concrete pipes that carry water from a central water supply to buildings and then with the pipes that carry sewage from the building to a water treatment plant.

Plumbers must be able to read blueprints and do simple carpentry work to make room for the pipes. They have to follow layout plans for the pipes and pay attention to building codes.

Working on new construction is one of the best jobs available to a plumber. But as you know, plumbers don't work only in clean new houses. You can probably remember a plumber disconnecting the pipe leading to your toilet or sink. Plumbers often work in tight places doing dirty jobs. As in other construction jobs, plumbers must be able to lift heavy materials and to work outdoors in cold and wet weather.

Education and Training

Many plumbers learn their trade through an apprenticeship. Apprenticeships are often supervised by members of various plumbers unions. If you decide on an apprenticeship, you will work four years for an established plumbing business. While on the job, you will also go to school part-time. You will take classes in drafting, blueprint reading, math, and plumbing codes. As an apprentice, you will earn about half as much as a fully trained plumber.

You can also train for this trade by taking a job as a plumber's helper. As a helper, you will not be required to go to school while you are training, but you may also not get the variety of experiences an apprentice does.

When you have finished your training as a plumber's

helper or apprentice, you must pass a test in order to receive your license to practice your trade. The test evaluates your knowledge of plumbing codes and your plumbing ability.

Career Opportunities and Salary

Opportunities for plumbers should be good in the next decade. Plumbers earn good money, too.

The plumbing trade also gives you the opportunity to work for yourself. Self-employed plumbers advertise their business and find their own jobs. Many people enjoy the independence of being their own boss.

ELECTRICIAN

If you think about it, you will realize how much we depend on electricity to make our lives run smoothly. From the alarm clock that wakes us in the morning to the video recorder that entertains us in the evening, electrical devices play an important part in our lives.

Electricians are among the people who keep these devices running smoothly for us. They may wire a tape deck in a car or hook up a mainframe computer in an office building. They may install wiring in a new house or update an old system in a factory. Electricians also repair motors and electrical appliances.

Electricians sometimes work in tight places or from the top of high ladders. They must take special care to avoid getting electric shocks. Electricians learn how to handle the responsibility of working with electricity, and they pay attention to safety rules.

As an electrician you will need good color vision. Electricians must match up colored wires according to a color-coded system. Being able to tell colors apart is a necessity in order to follow the wiring diagrams accurately.

Education and Training

Most electricians learn their trade through a four-year apprenticeship. Apprentices take classes in blueprint reading, math, and safety requirements. They also study construction codes that are part of the wiring trade. Then they apply their classroom experience to on-the-job situations. They learn to draw diagrams, set up circuits, and connect electrical systems. To get into an apprenticeship program, you have to be eighteen years old and have a high school diploma.

Electricians must have a license to work. To get their license they take a test on the National Electrical Code, electrical theory, and building codes for their area.

Career Opportunities and Salary

Electricians will have a good chance to get a job in the next decade. The Bureau of Labor Statistics says that the electrical trade is one of the craft occupations that will have the greatest number of job openings. Even so, the construction business is seasonal. Electricians may be laid off between major jobs.

Electricians also may decide to start their own electrical business. About 12 percent of all electricians are self-employed. If you are good at keeping the books and can relate well to people, you may enjoy applying your interest in electrical work to a business of your own.

Electricians earn about as much as plumbers.

FOR FURTHER READING

Chronicle Occupational Briefs. Moravia, N.Y.: Chronicle Guidance, 1987.

Hohn, Lynn, and Hohn, James. *Aim for a Job in the Construction Industry.* New York: Rosen, 1982.

Hopke, William E., ed. *The Encyclopedia of Careers and Vocational Guidance, VIII.* Chicago: Ferguson, 1984.

Jones, Marilyn. *Exploring Careers as a Carpenter.* New York: Rosen, 1985.

Jones, Marilyn. *Exploring Careers in Plumbing.* New York: Rosen, 1985.

Sumichrast, Michael, and McMahon, Charles P. *Opportunities in Building Construction.* Chicago: National Textbook, 1982.

Wood, Robert. *Opportunities in Electrical Trades.* Chicago: National Textbook, 1983.

U.S. Dept. of Labor, Bureau of Labor Statistics. *Occupational Outlook Handbook,* 1986–7.

8

SERVICE INDUSTRIES

"Love of the air" is what started Alexander on his career as an aircraft mechanic. This interest in flying attracted him to military service, and Alexander spent eight years in the air force, where he worked as a helicopter mechanic. An on-the-job training program prepared him for this job and also helped him find a job connected with flying when he returned to civilian life.

Currently Alexander works at a variety of jobs at an airport. He signals planes for landing and loads and unloads baggage. He does this job while working toward his Air Frame and Power Plant license. When he has this license, he can do maintenance work on any civilian aircraft in the United States.

Maintenance work on an aircraft is a very responsible job. You must pass a test to show that you do not use drugs. Aircraft companies want to prevent accidents caused by employees who use drugs or alcohol.

If you are interested in this kind of work, Alexander says, you should set your goals high and keep working

toward them. If you want a good job, it's worth working toward.

Service jobs are varied. They include work as teachers, nurses, and police officers. Firefighters, mechanics, and cooks are also employed in service industries.

Service jobs employ almost twice as many people as do goods-producing industries such as farming and manufacturing. In the future the trend toward employment in service occupations will continue. In fact, by 1995, 75 percent of all new jobs are expected to be in the service industries.

Although service jobs are plentiful, some are low paying. Child-care assistants, for example, often earn minimum wage. Waitresses and waiters may be hired at less than minimum wage. They depend on their tips to bring them a "living wage." However, skilled employees in the service industry are paid quite well. Mechanics, for example, earn good salaries. Jobs in high-tech services such as computer repair also pay well.

In this chapter, we will consider jobs based directly on a service to individuals. When you style hair, care for children, prepare food, or fix a car you are paid directly for the service you offer.

Alexander, an Air Force veteran, does a number of routine jobs at an airport while working toward a license that will allow him to do maintenance work on civilian aircraft.

MECHANIC

Do you like to "tinker" with engines? Can you keep an old car running smoothly? Do your friends call you "the person who can fix anything"? If you like to fix engines and repair machinery, you should consider becoming a mechanic.

Mechanics repair cars and trucks. They service farm machinery and aircraft. Mechanics usually choose one type of work. Some work on the diesel engines in semitrucks and heavy equipment, and some work on the gasoline engines in cars, lawn mowers, and other small machinery.

As a mechanic, you might work in a service station repairing cars or at an airport maintaining planes. Some mechanics make service calls to start stalled cars or tow in vehicles that have broken down.

Most mechanics are called in to fix broken equipment, but mechanics may also routinely check equipment to make sure it is running right. Aircraft mechanics, for example, routinely take apart plane engines and check for worn parts. Parts that show signs of wear may be replaced before they actually break down. The mechanics help prevent problems for the plane.

Mechanics must notice little things. When an engine does not run properly, mechanics use testing equipment to find weak connections, cracks in the casing, or worn parts.

Mechanics use logical thinking skills to decide on what repairs are necessary. They put all the information they have together and decide what to fix and what to replace in order to get the machine running smoothly again.

Mechanics often work in cold, noisy places. They may repair an airplane on a windy runway or work in a garage where loud machines run all day.

Skilled mechanics are always in demand.

Being a mechanic can be dirty work, and it is often hard at the end of the day to get rid of the grease of the mechanic's trade. For people who have to work with machines, however, the satisfaction of watching a "well oiled" engine run smoothly makes up for whatever discomfort there may be in the working conditions.

Education and Training

You can start preparing for a job as a mechanic in high school by taking courses in math, mechanical drawing, and computer science. A knowledge of electronics and computers is important to mechanics today because a lot of machinery has electronic parts.

Some automotive mechanics start out as gas station attendants, but getting some specialized training is a good idea. Working on motors as a hobby is also a good way to prepare yourself for a mechanic's job.

Vocational schools offer training programs that vary from six months to two years. You can also get mechanics training in the military.

Enrolling in an apprenticeship is another way to learn this trade. Apprenticeship programs last three to four years and have both on-the-job experience and classroom instruction.

Employers may also send their mechanics to factory training schools. In these schools, the mechanic learns the special needs of a particular product. For example, a mechanic may attend a school to repair Fords or Hondas (or whatever) if the boss has a dealership for those cars.

Some jobs require more training than others. An aircraft mechanic, for example, must be licensed by the government to work on planes. You will need at least eighteen months of work experience before you are eligible to take the licensing exam. Some training programs can be substituted for work experience.

Career Opportunities and Salary

The average mechanic earns a good salary, with aircraft mechanics earning considerably more. Mechanics work 40 to 48 hours a week and may belong to a union such as the International Association of Machinists and Aerospace Workers.

As a mechanic, you will have a good chance of getting a job, especially if you choose work as an automotive mechanic.

CHILD-CARE ASSISTANT

Do you like working with young children? Do you enjoy watching them play together and helping them learn new things?

Child-care assistants work in day-care centers and nursery schools. They help preschool teachers plan and direct activities for young children. They lead sing-alongs, help children with art projects, and organize games. They also help children learn to play together and develop good eating and resting habits.

You will need a lot of energy to keep up with the children, but you will also be rewarded with the enthusiasm and friendship of young children.

Education and Training

Most child-care assistants have some education beyond high school. Vocational schools offer short courses in child development, and some have one-year diploma programs in child care. Your high school may even offer a course in child care.

In these programs you may study child development and nutrition. You will learn how to talk to young children and how to discipline them. You may also learn how to plan games and art projects for preschoolers.

If the state in which you want to work requires licensing of day-care centers, you will need to meet the licensing requirements—usually one or two short courses in child

Childcare assistants need a lot of energy
to keep up with young children, but they
are rewarded with the loving friendship
of their students.

development—before you can work in a licensed day-care center.

Career Opportunities and Salary

You will find lots of work in this field. As more mothers join the work force, the need for child-care workers increases.

Although job openings in child care are numerous, the pay is low and the chances for advancement are limited. Many day-care workers make the minimum wage. If you want to advance in this field, you will probably need a college degree to qualify as a head teacher. However, the low salaries may improve in the future as more people begin to use day-care centers and as the prestige of child-care workers increases.

CHEF/COOK

Do you like to cook? Do you like to try new recipes and experiment with new ideas? Are you pleased when people enjoy eating what you have prepared? You can earn a good income with your cooking and baking skills by working as a chef or a cook.

Chefs and cooks prepare different kinds of foods depending upon where they work. In fine restaurants the chef cooks special main dishes and desserts "from scratch." The restaurant's reputation depends to a great extent on the chef's ability to prepare tasty meals. People visit the restaurant because they have heard about the delicious breads, salads, or seafoods the chef prepares. In smaller, less specialized restaurants the chef usually prepares simpler meals and may depend in part on frozen foods and mixes.

In large hotels and restaurants chefs may specialize. They may prepare only desserts or stir-fried foods, for example. In small family-owned restaurants, on the other hand, they may be responsible for preparing many different foods at one time.

Chefs and cooks also find jobs cooking in hospitals and school cafeterias in which they prepare food for large groups of people. In these jobs they pay attention to how well balanced and nutritious the meal is as well as to how good it tastes. They may also work as caterers or start their own business.

Chefs must be able to work under pressure. Hungry people want good food quickly. Restaurant managers want the food to be prepared in the same way all the time. As in other service occupations, the job of chef can be demanding but rewarding. The satisfaction of knowing that your customers enjoyed the meal you prepared can be worth the stress you might have felt in preparing it.

Education and Training

You can train for a chef's job in a variety of ways. Until recently many chefs learned their trade by taking a job as a kitchen helper and working their way up to chef or head cook.

Now, however, many technical institutes and junior colleges offer courses in food preparation. These courses

Growth in the restaurant industry has created a large demand for experienced chefs.

may last a few months or fill an entire two-year program. If you choose to enter one of these programs you will learn how to prepare food and plan menus. You will also learn how to handle food in a sanitary way according to public health standards.

Another way to train for a chef's job is to enroll in an apprenticeship program. Apprenticeships in this field are usually for three years, during which time you will take classes in cooking while you work in the field. Apprenticeships give you the chance to use what you have learned in class in actual job situations.

Another source of training is through the armed services. If you are thinking about entering and are interested in food preparation, you should consider signing up for classes when you enlist.

Career Opportunities and Salary

An interest in cooking can lead you to a good job. Openings for chefs will be plentiful in the next ten years and career advancement opportunities are excellent. The average salary for chefs is quite low, but top chefs earn good money. If you can establish a reputation as a chef, your earning power should be excellent.

HAIRSTYLIST

Hairstylists—also called cosmetologists—cut and style hair. They give permanents and scalp treatments according to their clients' requests. They may suggest hair coloring or hairstyles that would look best on their customers. They show their customers how to apply makeup and may give manicures and facials.

Today many hairstylists work in department stores or malls, where they style both men's and women's hair. Two interesting things about hairstyling often attract people to this occupation. First, it is a good opportunity to be self-employed. About one-half of all hairstylists own their own shops. Second, it is also a good source of part-time work. Many hairstylists work part time; they find this job a good way to combine a job with raising a family, for example.

Hairstylists must be good listeners. They need to be able to follow directions carefully in order to give their clients the look they want. Since many clients enjoy talking to their hairstylists as much as they enjoy having their hair styled, stylists need to listen sympathetically and carry on friendly conversations.

Although cosmetologists usually work in attractive, pleasant places, they do have to stand for long periods of time. They also often work evenings and weekends because that is the only time many of their clients can keep appointments.

Education and Training

If you choose hairstyling as a career, you should enroll in a cosmetology course. This usually takes six months to a year to complete. During the course you will practice haircutting and styling on your classmates and on clients who come to the school.

A few states also offer apprenticeship programs in which you work in a shop with an experienced hairstylist. Apprentices learn from watching and helping the cosmetologists in the shop. When you have completed the course you will take a state licensing exam. Each state gives its own test. On the test you will be asked to answer written questions and to show how well you style hair.

When you pass the test you are licensed to work as a hairstylist in that state. If you move to another state, you may need to take another test.

Career Opportunities and Salary

Most hairstylists begin their careers working for someone else. The employer provides the work area, and the hairstylists provide the scissors, curling iron, and other styling equipment they use. The shop's owner and the hairstylist split the fees. Your income will depend on how many clients you have.

Hairstylists also make money from tips. If you own your own shop or have a lot of business, or work on wealthy customers, you will earn much more.

Career opportunities look good for cosmetologists in the next decade thanks to an increased number of women in the job market and more men going to beauty shops for hairstyling.

FOR FURTHER READING

Chronicle Occupational Briefs. Moravia, N.Y.: Chronicle Guidance, 1987.

Gearhart, Susan. *Opportunities in Beauty Culture.* Chicago: National Textbook, 1983.

Hopke, William E., ed. *The Encyclopedia of Careers and Vocational Guidance, VIII.* Chicago: Ferguson, 1984.

Ispa, Jean. *Exploring Careers in Child Care Services.* New York: Rosen, 1983.

Opportunities in Food Services. Chicago: National Textbook, 1983.

"Spotlight on Service: Where the Jobs Are." *Occupational Outlook Quarterly,* Summer 1985, pp. 2–3.

U.S. Dept. of Labor, Bureau of Labor Statistics. *Occupational Outlook Handbook,* 1986–7.

9

PLANNING FOR YOUR FUTURE

You may have read about Steve Wozniak, the computer whiz who, after earning a fortune in the computer business, returned to college to earn a bachelor's degree. Although he was very successful in the work world, he wanted to complete a college education.

You too may be successful in the work world but decide that you want a college degree. "Going back to school" is becoming an increasingly popular thing to do. Unlike our parents and grandparents, who may have stayed in the same occupation their entire working lives, most of us will change jobs at least several times during our lifetimes. Education will be an ongoing process, with about 4 percent of the work force in school at any one time. Most of us will return to school once every ten years to retrain for a new job or update our skills for a job we are doing. Think of the training you receive now as the first step in a series of rewarding career opportunities.

From the time you take your first job, keep a record of your work experiences. Save certificates from short courses you take while on the job and memos you receive from supervisors commending you for work well done. Compile a list of duties you perform on the job and skills you acquire. These job descriptions show the variety of tasks you are capable of doing.

Put all this material together in a folder called a portfolio. When you request admission to a college, take the portfolio with you. Most colleges and universities give credit for "life experiences." That means if you have written many reports and memos on your job, you may be granted credit for a technical writing course.

You may also be able to "test out" of some classes because of your job experience. For example, if you have worked as a welder and can show that you know how to weld expertly, you may be given credit for a course in basic welding.

You can also get credit for technical school or junior college classes. Many universities allow you to apply your entire associate degree toward their four-year program. That means you have two years of college completed before you even enter a program. With a combination of credit for your associate degree and pertinent life experiences, you may need only a year or so of study to earn a bachelor's degree.

Whatever decisions you make now, remember that work in the future offers a variety of choices. Don't think that the job you select now need be the work you will do for the rest of your life. Choose your work and educational opportunities carefully and continue to build on them throughout your working life. Take advantage of opportunities for education and retraining and you will enjoy a challenging, rewarding work life.

BIBLIOGRAPHY

Allen, Jeffrey G. *How to Turn an Interview into a Job.* New York: Simon and Schuster, 1983.

Angel, Dr. Juvenal L. *The Complete Résumé Book and Job-Getters Guide.* New York: Pocket, 1980.

Arco Editorial Board. *How to Pass Employment Tests,* 7th ed. New York: Arco, 1982.

Bostwisk, Burdette, E. *How to Find the Job You've Always Wanted.* New York: Wiley, 1980.

Figler, Howard E. *The Complete Job-Search Handbook: All the Skills You Need to Get Any Job and Have a Good Time Doing It.* New York: Holt, Rinehart, 1980.

Friendenberg, Joan E. *Finding a Job in the USA.* Chicago: National Textbook, 1986.

Holtz, H. *Beyond the Résumé: How to Land the Job You Want.* New York: McGraw-Hill, 1984.

Jackson, Tom. *How to Get the Job You Want in 28 Days.* New York: Dutton, 1982.

Schmidt, Peggy J. *Making It on Your First Job: When You're Young, Inexperienced and Ambitious.* New York: Avon, 1981.

Truitt, John. *Telesearch: Direct Dial the Best Job of Your Life.* New York: Facts on File, 1983.

Washington, Tom. *Résumé Power: Selling Yourself on Paper.* Washington, D.C.: Mount Vernon Press, 1985.

INDEX